Time Management

The Importance Of Mental Health: Unleash Your Full Potential: The Enhancement Of Well-Being Through Effective Time Management

(Methods For Achieving Optimal Concentration And Productivity Through Laser-Like Focus)

Felton Valencia

TABLE OF CONTENT

Workflow 1

Delaying 12

Forgetting Is Not A Negative Thing. 24

How To Properly And Efficiently Organise Your Time. 36

Time Theft: The Effects Of Postponement 51

Setting Smart, Visible Goals 61

Getting Input 76

Outsourcing And Consolidation 88

Taking Command Of Your Life: Techniques For Achieving Your Objectives. 121

Workflow

Accordingly, the first step in the workflow is to capture all the goals and commitments one has. Once you have captured all the essential things that need to be done, process what they are and what they represent. If you are of the opinion that a certain task can be discarded, score it off from your list. This is when you enter the second stage of the workflow. Upon clarifying, you will have a clear idea about each task on the list. You will have an exact figure on the tasks that require your action.

The third step in the workflow is to organize them accordingly. Group them into similar tasks. For example, all household chores can be clubbed together, while errands that require you to go out can be clubbed separately. Prepare separate lists of similar activities.

The fourth step in the workflow is to reflect on our tasks. This is nothing but to review them from time to time. This will also help you identify those tasks that are yet to be completed. Update your lists after each review. This way, both your list as well as your mind is clear from things that have already been completed, and the entire focus can be on the things that require completion.

The fifth and final step in the workflow is to engage. This simply means putting your plan into action. Look at your lists and start working on them with confidence and energy.

Hence, this method helps us to focus on the things that need to be done in the short run, thereby preparing us for the tasks that need to be completed in the long run.

Summary

What knowledge have we gained?

You've reached the book's final chapter!!!!!! Best wishes. In case any of you missed it, we will quickly recap everything that was previously covered in this chapter.

We first discussed the idea of time management and the various ways that people understood it. We delved deeper into the idea that time management is entirely dependent on your perspective and way of living. We then concentrated on the causes of time management issues. I provided numerous examples and pointers on how to resolve the situation.

We talked about time management strategies in the middle of the book. I provided fifty useful pointers and advice that were targeted at the current issue. We dissected those clues and looked into the significance in more detail.

Then, we talked about the various methods we may use to schedule visits with our loved ones. Once more, I've given you a list of useful illustrations and advice. After that, we talked about how to make the much-needed change in your life and how it can better meet your needs. Next, we talked about general life organization strategies. In addition, I gave you examples and practice exercises.

We concentrated on additional time management examples, crucial things to keep in mind, and practical advice near the end of the book. We talked about the various ways that people see time and how you can choose how you view it overall. We talked about the myths around time and how, ultimately, it is detrimental to see time as your opponent.

Throughout the whole book, we discussed the concept of time, how it affects our lives, and how we can make changes to take charge of our destiny. I talked about strategies and approaches to help you lead happier lives. Along the way, I made some suggestions that ought to have inspired you to improve your time management.

Ultimately, the idea behind this book was to provide you with a notion that you may then modify on your own. Of course, this book can help you get started, but in the end, you have to put in the work. The remainder is left to you. You must maintain your routines, develop healthy habits, and give yourself space to breathe. It really is all up to you.

Thus, keep this in mind the next time you find yourself racing against the clock, stressed out about time, or dreading something. You possess the ability to alter things. You possess the ability to change things. Everything is up to you. I've given you some pointers, advice, and samples. You now have to put in the remaining work after I gave you the motivation you required.

Refuse to be controlled by time. Do not let time elapse on you. Don't let poor time management drive you to neglect your friends and family. Develop your organizing abilities, form virtuous habits, and change the world.

Ten Enchanted Minutes

In ten minutes, what can you do? Refocus your energies, move and stretch, have a nutritious snack, make plans for the afternoon or evening, and so much more. In this chapter, you will discover more about how ten minutes well-spent can significantly impact your day. Additionally, you will discover how to determine whether your ten-minute breaks are being used for constructive purposes or are being squandered on pointless activities and diversions. By the time this chapter ends, you ought to be inspired to do something worthwhile with your 10 minutes and have enough ideas to make that time effective.

Go on to the subsequent assignment.

When someone finishes work 10 minutes sooner than anticipated, this is what they usually do. They frequently carry over those 10 minutes to the following activity, finishing even earlier and with an extra fifteen or twenty minutes of leisure time. If you're in the mood to work and don't want to lose the momentum you've built up at work, then just go through your to-do list and complete the jobs faster than the timetable indicates. Not only will you feel accomplished and confident when your work is done, but you'll also get at least 30 minutes to yourself before the next round of errands and responsibilities arrive.

2. Go through a book.

Pick up the book that's currently on your shelf and continue where you left off. If the book you selected is an anthology, open it to any page at random and read the poem or tale that appears. Reading helps us learn new things and expands our creativity. Every time we pick up a book, we have the opportunity to travel, experience new things, and meet new people.

3. Compose a journal entry.

If reading isn't your thing, perhaps writing down your thoughts or your day will help you unwind and prepare for your next assignment. Writing about anything at all is difficult, even though it can be helpful. What benefit does journaling offer further? If you ever become well-known, your notebook might be the key to writing a best-selling memoir that admirers will be clamouring to read, or you might just find pleasure in perusing old, worn-out journal pages as a way to reflect on your life.

4. Scribble and doodle.

Why not get a piece of paper, some pens, or even some crayons and use different colours to express your weariness as a simple way to decompress? Similar to journaling, doodling and scribbling relieve tension, revitalize you, and occasionally provide the inspiration you need to finish that crucial assignment.

5. Take in some tunes.

The language of the soul is music. Thus, put in your earbuds and let your favourite music blast away all of your stress whenever you feel too exhausted or depressed to carry out your schedule. If you'd like, you can even sing along.

6. Give your aching muscles a stretch.

While you're getting up from your chair and moving around your home or office, stretch your arms and legs. To help your blood flow and oxygen levels return to normal, take a short stroll to and from the sandwich shop or coffee shop.

7. Snack on something.

Take out the sandwich that your significant other made just for you, and enjoy every bite of it. Alternatively, it might be preferable to split the sandwich with a coworker who is just as hungry and spend ten minutes catching up. You will have had a wonderful, brief talk in addition to a pleasant supper together.

Now, take note of the fact that "Check your email," "Look at your Facebook notifications," and "Take a nap" were not on this list. It is rarely productive to check your Facebook and email notifications (unless you frequently receive urgent or critical communications). Actually, staring at a computer with an Internet connection might deter you from effectively managing your time and even persuade you to turn that ten-minute break into a half-hour or more.

Postpone using social media until after you've completed all the essential tasks. Ten-minute naps can sometimes be problematic. Ten-minute naps won't likely wake you up feeling more alert; instead, they'll likely make you feel even sleepier or give you a headache. When you have at least twenty or thirty minutes to spare, save the naps.

Delaying

One of the most frequent barriers to productivity is procrastination, which can result in missed deadlines and needless stress. This chapter will address the underlying causes of procrastination and offer solutions.

1. We might put off doing anything indefinitely if we're concerned we won't do it well. In order to get over this, we need to change the way we

view failure. Consider failure an opportunity to develop and learn rather than a bad result. Aim for progress rather than perfection because perfectionism can be a disguised form of procrastination.

2. Lack of motivation: This is another factor that contributes to procrastination. It might be challenging to begin something when we lack motivation. Try creating more manageable objectives or segmenting a task into manageable steps to get around this. As you proceed, acknowledge your accomplishments and treat yourself when you reach your objectives.

3. Overwhelm: Feeling overburdened by a task might occasionally be the cause of procrastination. Whenever an assignment

appears too large or intricate, it might be challenging to know where to begin. Try dividing the work into smaller, more doable chunks to get around this. Make a to-do list with clear assignments and due dates, then work through each item on the list one at a time.

4. Distractions: Another important factor in procrastination is distractions. Distractions like social media and email notifications might make it hard to concentrate on the current task at hand. To get around this, try scheduling particular times to check social media or email and disable notifications while you're working intently.

5. Accountability: Taking responsibility for your actions is one of the best strategies to stop procrastinating. To assist you in staying on course, look for a group or accountability

partner. Talk to someone else about your objectives and advancements, and solicit their encouragement and support.

By comprehending the underlying reasons behind procrastination and putting tactics in place to combat it, you can boost your output and accomplish your objectives.

We'll talk about work-life balance and how to strike a healthy balance between work and other facets of your life in the next part.

Explore the psychological underpinnings of why humans procrastinate

Many people have been fascinated and perplexed by the procrastination riddle throughout history. We must go more into the psychological underpinnings of this intriguing phenomenon in order to fully understand its complexity. The psychological motivators that lie beyond the surface causes of procrastination can shed light on the intricate relationships, behaviours, and motivations that occur within our minds. This chapter deconstructs a complicated picture of human conduct by examining the psychological elements at play that underlie our tendency to put things off.

Fear of not succeeding and self-doubt

Often, the dread of failing lies at the core of procrastination. The mere fear of falling short of one's own or other people's expectations might set off a psychological response that makes people put off doing a task entirely. It's possible for the dread of failing to become so intense that it seems simpler to put off a task indefinitely rather than face the possible frustration of falling short of perfection. Alongside the dread of failing, self-doubt contributes to procrastination. Procrastination on jobs requiring effort or ability is more common among those who have self-doubt or mistrust their abilities. The overwhelming barrier of the subconscious thought that they would not be able to handle the issue is what keeps people in the procrastination loop.

Poor self-confidence

The term "self-efficacy," which was first used by psychologist Albert Bandura, describes a person's confidence in their capacity to finish activities or produce desired outcomes. Procrastination is more common in those with poor self-efficacy because they believe their efforts are in vain and their abilities are insufficient. A self-fulfilling prophecy may result from this lack of confidence, whereby their delay serves as a confirmation of their perception of their incompetence. Fascinatingly, self-efficacy can vary by region. A person may procrastinate in some parts of their life because they feel unqualified, yet they may feel competent in other areas. Procrastination can be fought by strengthening one's feeling of self-efficacy via mastery experiences and encouraging feedback.

Trend of Instant Gratification

The allure of rapid gratification greatly influences human behaviour. Our evolutionary past, in which survival has depended on collecting resources rapidly, is the cause of this instant reward bias. This propensity can cause us to put short-term gratification ahead of long-term objectives in the modern environment. Tasks that promise rewards later on compete with instant gratification activities like scrolling through social media, viewing movies, or indulging in comfort food. An inclination for fast gratification is reinforced by the brain's pleasure centres, which react more strongly to rewards that arrive right away. Because of this, it may be challenging for us to focus our attention and exert the necessary effort on things that have broad advantages, which eventually causes us to put them off.

Discounting Time and Trends

Time discounting is a cognitive phenomenon where benefits that occur later in life are given less weight. We tend to choose the present over the future due to this bias, which makes it challenging to work on projects that will only be worthwhile after a substantial time and effort commitment. This cognitive distortion is closely linked to the present bias phenomenon, which favours immediate gratification above long-term advantages. Procrastination arises from a contradiction between our current orientation and the needs of tasks that require delayed gratification. We find it difficult to weigh the possible benefits of a quest's future benefits against the difficulty of embarking on it now, so we choose temporary comfort over long-term benefits.

The Effect of Zeigarnik

According to a psychological theory known as the Zeigarnik effect, we tend to recall interrupted or incomplete tasks more vividly than finished ones. This phenomenon puts mental strain on us, bringing the unfinished business of finding closure back to our attention. The Zeigarnik effect can encourage someone to finish a task, but if it is postponed repeatedly, it can also cause procrastination. Ironically, the mental weight of unfinished business accumulates as duties are postponed, leading to tension and anxiety. This pain can eventually become too much for us to handle, which drives us to finish chores in order to relieve our mental tension.

Postpone Making a Decision

Making decisions can be stressful, which can lead to procrastination. People often put off making decisions when presented with difficult options or novel jobs because they are afraid of choosing the incorrect option. Decision delay is the term for this kind of delay, where people put off making decisions in order to prevent unfavourable outcomes. The need to feel in control of the outcome is the root cause of decision delay. However, when crucial decisions are postponed or avoided completely, this propensity can result in lost chances and untapped potential.

Substitute Award

When people swap out an internal task reward for an external incentive or reward, this is known as reward substitution. For instance, a student may put off preparing for an exam until the very last minute, hoping that the stress of a deadline will instil a sense of enthusiasm and urgency in him. This external pressure momentarily replaces the natural satisfaction of mastering the content. Reward replacement prolongs a cycle of depending on outside triggers to start action, even when it can result in a last-minute productivity boost. Developing an inherent motivation that surpasses the desire for outside benefits is the difficult part.

The Fallacy of Planning

A cognitive bias known as planning error occurs when people underestimate the amount of time, money, and effort needed to do a task. Because people tend to overestimate their ability to finish activities more quickly than they actually can, this overly optimistic assessment can result in poor time management. Consequently, individuals could put off beginning assignments, thinking they have ample time to finish the work alone as the due date draws near. Lack of knowledge or experience with the current task frequently makes scheduling problems worse. It is necessary to implement time management techniques and gain a more precise understanding of task requirements in order to overcome this bias.

b. Give out assignments carefully

The princes made it their mission to identify the cause of the issue. They realised that they were better suited to complete the work. To find out the reason, they could have given their assistants the duty. The assistants would have returned in the first or second stage if they had completed it.

We should utilise delegation of work extensively as it is a valuable time management strategy. But the only things we should assign are those that others are better suited to do and that we don't need to do ourselves. With the help of delegation, we can allocate our time more wisely to the duties that we are most capable of handling and assign the ones that others can complete competently.

Forgetting Is Not A Negative Thing.

This story's hero lost its name. Naturally, I haven't yet encountered a (well) individual who can't remember his name. However, there is nothing wrong with occasionally forgetting certain things. It affects every one of us. We overlook the birthdays of our spouses. We can't remember the boss's name. Nothing wrong with it, but you should also make an effort to strengthen your memory. We can use different applications and devices to help us remember significant events like birthdays, but there are a lot of things we should teach our brains to remember.

Important things are always better off being noted on a computer, smartphone, or journal. Occasionally, a crazy idea will occur to you, sounding creative at the time, but it will fade away in a few hours. Successful people often capture such haphazard thoughts for further processing. We can store five to nine thoughts in our short-term memory, according to psychologists. That means that, on average, you only get the last seven ideas that cross your mind. Something falls out when you add the eighth item to the list. While memory is expensive, ideas are cheap[6].

Keep a tiny pocketbook, diary, or journal—whatever size and format works best for you—with you at all times to record your thoughts. When I sleep, I keep my little pocketbook close to my bed. From what I've heard, Einstein wrote out $E=mc^2$ when he was asleep. When we wake up, we are not as nerdy as Einstein to recall them. If you are more at ease using your smartphone, you can also use digital apps like Google Keep. The goal is to record all of those sporadic, brilliant ideas. Once these concepts are written down, go over them frequently and eliminate any that don't seem useful. Put anything worthwhile to investigate on your to-do list. Once every three months, completely reset your list.

It is possible to train memory, which brings us to our next point. Don't be hard on yourself for being forgetful. You are admitting to a lasting loss by doing this. You can acknowledge the issue and make an effort to resolve it. We can train our memory in the same way as we would any other skill, like riding a motorbike. Numerous books exist regarding memory enhancement. During the weekend, pick one up and read it. But everything demands work. Make it a regular goal to sharpen your memory. Strive to commit crucial dates, phone numbers, etc., to memory. Have faith in your ability to enhance your memory; this will bring about several improvements.

The Hungry Crow

A thirsty crow swooped across the fields in search of water on a sweltering July day. It looked far and wide, but I was unable to discover any drinkable water. The crow eventually became quite feeble and gave up on life. Its attention was suddenly drawn to a water jug beneath the tree. It descended vertically to check for the presence of water. Yes, the crow was finally able to see some water in the jug!

The crow attempted to insert his head into the pitcher. Unfortunately, the jug's neck was too small. Then, in an attempt to allow the water to pour out, it tilted the jug, but it was too heavy. The crow took some time to reflect. It looked around and noticed a few pebbles. At that moment, something clicked, and it began to pick up the stones one by one and deposit them all into the jug. The water level continued to rise as the jug filled with more and more pebbles. The water level soon rose to a safe level for drinking. The crow's scheme had succeeded! It may finally find some water to drink.

I must have heard this story a thousand times; it's one of the most well-known. But each time, it sounds fresh. This is the first tale that my 2.5-year-old daughter has learned and performed so skillfully.

Accept Minimalism

Have you ever had the feeling that there aren't enough hours in the day to complete your tasks? I understand the emotion; I promise.

However, I've just lately come to understand the time-saving and clutter-reducing benefits of minimalism. It's a way of life that goes far beyond fashion. The goal is to live a simpler life and focus on the things that matter most.

In a congested world, minimalism is a breath of fresh air. Accepting it will help you declutter your life and establish a calm atmosphere that will give you more time and mental clarity. You'll be able to concentrate on the things that truly offer you joy and fulfilment instead of wasting hours cleaning and organising your belongings.

The way minimalism streamlines your schedule is one of my favourite aspects of it. You may make your most important commitments and activities your top priority by deliberately choosing how to use your time. When you stop feeling like you have to do everything at once, it's as if a weight has been lifted off your shoulders. You are capable of building a balanced, contented existence that keeps you from becoming overburdened and exhausted.

The remarkable advantage of minimalism is its ability to lessen decision fatigue. You have less stuff, fewer obligations, and fewer choices to make. If there were just a few options available, just think of how much simpler it would be to make decisions.

Adopting a minimalist lifestyle will help you reach your objectives and experience greater joy in your daily life, whether your goals are to lower stress, increase productivity, or build a more satisfying life. It simplifies your life and frees you up to concentrate on the things that really matter, much like a warm hug. Minimalism can greatly improve your time management.

Practice: Living Simply for Maximum Impact

You may live a more minimalistic existence by cutting back on clutter and improving your time management skills with this exercise. You'll be well on your way to a more contented, organised, and joyful existence by taking these easy steps:

Step 1: Set a 15-minute timer and play some energetic music. Examine your belongings during this time and get rid of anything you don't need or use. Start small, like a closet or drawer, and work your way around your house little by bit.

Step 2: Ask yourself, "Do I use this regularly?" when you look through your belongings. Do I feel happy about this? If the response to any of these questions is "no," think about selling, giving the item away, or donating it.

Step 3: Make plans to take stuff out of your house once you've determined which ones you no longer need. Arrange for a yard sale, arrange for a donation pick-up, or deliver items to a nearby charity.

Step 4: Apply the principle of "one in, one out." Try getting rid of one old item for every new one you bring into your house. This may aid in preventing the first accumulation of clutter.

Step 5: Make your calendar simpler by figuring out which commitments and activities don't make you happy or are in line with your ideals. Think about declining these activities and focusing just on the ones that are really important to you.

You'll have more time and energy to devote to the things that really matter in life with your newfound minimalist perspective. Savour the liberty and happiness that come with leading a simple, clutter-free life, and welcome the limitless opportunities that lie ahead of you.

Streamline Your Work Procedures

It might be stressful to attempt to keep everything under control and manage everything you have on your plate. You shouldn't panic, though, because streamlining your workflow will help you become more productive and less chaotic. You'll feel more accomplished and less anxious if you do this.

Take a thorough "work inventory" and list all of your duties, responsibilities, and projects as the first stage in this process. Although it may appear overwhelming, this is the most effective way to see exactly what needs to be done. Remember to breathe during this procedure and take breaks as required. The goal of this workout is to support you rather than cause you more tension.

The next stage after creating your job inventory is to analyse it and determine which tasks are significant, non-essential, and necessary. This is the location of the magic! You'll be able to determine which tasks are essential to your job, which ones can be assigned, and which ones don't really add anything to it. With this newfound understanding, you can make a calendar that emphasises crucial and significant chores and represents your priorities.

When you're organising your calendar, remember to cross out unnecessary activities and distractions. We are all aware of how difficult it is to maintain concentration in chaotic situations or when alerts appear nonstop. Thus, inhale deeply, pour yourself a cup of tea, and get your workstation in order. When you're done, you'll feel a lot more at ease and concentrated.

You need to take breaks for both your health and productivity. Stretch, go for a stroll, or practise meditation to help you decompress and refuel. It's equally crucial to look for yourself as it is to look after your work.

Keep track of your progress, and remember to celebrate your victories. Whatever the size of the accomplishment, it ought to be recognised and honoured. Additionally, tracking your development helps you stay motivated by allowing you to see how far you've come. Tracking and celebrating your victories will give you the drive to cross your goals' finish line, just like a marathon runner who records every mile and takes joy in their progress.

The key to optimising your work process is striking a balance, concentrating on what matters, and caring for yourself.

How To Properly And Efficiently Organise Your Time.

The three P's of Time Management are important strategies for efficiently managing your time. "Do you ever feel like you can't keep up with all the work you have to do or that you're overwhelmed by the amount of work you have to do?

You can focus on a variety of areas to improve your time-management skills. Knowing how you spend your time can be a good place to start. Once you've identified the harmful behaviours, the next step is to learn how to change them. Here are some ideas and strategies you can use to use the three P's of time management—planning, prioritising, and performing—to feel more productive and get more done.

- Organising

A well-known proverb goes, "If you don't plan, you're planning to fail." You won't know what has to be done to complete a project successfully if you don't plan. You might not be as prepared as you should be, encounter unforeseen difficulties, and miss deadlines; as a result, your reputation might be in danger. That could make you feel stressed, disoriented, and overwhelmed. Planning is important, even though the results might not be seen right away. Consider the costs associated with not being ready.

Plan your next day for at least fifteen minutes at the conclusion of the day. In this manner, you'll feel as though you've accomplished what you needed to at the end of the day and wake up knowing exactly what has to be done. Writing everything down and not holding anything in your head is the first step. Write everything down on a sheet of paper or an Excel spreadsheet, whichever is most convenient for you. Don't forget to incorporate your regular responsibilities into your daily schedule. Be realistic when estimating the time needed for a task and assign a certain amount of time for it.

Additionally, keep in mind to keep your activities small and focused on only one at a time. The email is too long to complete; will you be working on the content, layout, or design? Not the outcome, but each step must be recorded in writing.

You've now listed all the tasks you need to complete and allocated the necessary time for them. What comes next? Which task do we complete initially? Since the day only has so many hours, we should spend them on the tasks that will benefit us the most in order to be more productive. That suggests that you must set priorities, decide which tasks need to be completed, and set those priorities appropriately.

Setting priorities

What would be the most significant item on the list if I could only choose one? Which assignments would yield the highest return on my time investment?

Once the most crucial task has been identified, look for the next, third, and so on, keeping in mind the time allocated for each. You can group your tasks into other categories, which could help you prioritise, but you should focus most of your attention on the first and second categories listed below:

Vital and urgent: A prompt reaction is necessary for these occupations. These tasks must be completed immediately because they are urgent, but keep in mind that if you constantly putting out fires, you won't have time for other essential but non-urgent tasks.

Significant but not urgent: These calls for action must be taken eventually, even though it is not necessary to do so today. The majority of your time should be spent in this section.

Important but not urgent: These tasks are not very important, but they do require quick attention. These appear when you start answering yes to too many requests from other people or when you start to get interrupted.

Not critical nor urgent: While these tasks are worthwhile in the long run, they are typical examples of busy labour that is frequently distracting, like cleaning your desk and sending emails. You feel busy with these responsibilities.

Time lost: Where else would you rather spend your time? Is it worthwhile to complete this task? Is it assignable?

● Acting

You must act when you have prioritised and made a plan! This suggests that you must concentrate on a single task until it is completed in its entirety! It must be completed without any breaks or distractions. Put an end to your email and turn off your mobile device; get rid of any distractions you know you frequently encounter. Your output will increase as a result, as will the calibre and volume of your work. You'll be amazed at how much you can do if you focus on completing one task at a time! Remember to follow your energy, or how you feel, and do important tasks when you are at your most alert and active.

Recall that the three Ps are Performance, Prioritisation, and Planning. And never forget to change how you use the time you have now if you are unable to find more of it."

Here are some more time-management strategies that work:

● Clearly define goals

Set measurable and reachable goals for yourself. Use the SMART approach when setting goals. To put it simply, make sure the goals you set are Specific, Measurable, Achievable, Relevant, and Timely.

Establish a deadline for completing a task.

Setting deadlines for tasks you want to complete makes you more productive and focused. You may be able to see potential problems before they arise if you take a little extra time to determine how much time you need to dedicate to each task. In this manner, you can create plans for handling them.

Let's take an example where you have five reviews to write and a meeting to attend. However, you understand that in the short amount of time left before the conference, you can only finish four of them. You might be able to just hire someone else to post one of the reviews if you find out about this information well in advance. However, you might not have realised your time crunch until an hour before the meeting if you hadn't bothered to do a time check on your duties beforehand. At that point, it might be more harder to find someone to assign one of the assessments to, and it might also be harder for them to fit the job into their schedule.

● Pause in between tasks

Maintaining focus and motivation is more difficult while working on multiple tasks at once. Between jobs, give yourself a break to refresh your mind and revitalise.

● Think about the best days to dedicate to specific projects. To discuss cash flow, for instance, you might need to schedule a meeting for a day when you know the business CFO will be available.

● Get rid of unnecessary chores and activities

Reducing extracurricular activities and jobs is essential. Decide what is important and what needs your focus. Reducing unnecessary chores and activities allows you to devote more of your time to truly important things.

● Lack of Sleep

An adult needs to sleep for seven to nine hours every night on average. Nonetheless, a lot of people get less than that, sometimes much less. One of the main causes of this problem is ineffective time management. When you have a lot on your plate and are surrounded by distractions, it can be quite difficult to get enough sleep.

● Physical Medical Conditions

Effective time management is essential to our physical well-being. Studies have shown that people with better time management are typically more active. We must learn to balance the amount of time we spend on different interests if we want to live a healthy life. Using time wisely is the first step in this.

● Adverse Financial Impact

Money is time. You usually make more money if you invest time in income-producing endeavours. As easy as that. Those with good time management abilities typically experience positive financial effects, even if it's not always easy to spot these kinds of activities.

● Insufficient self-improvement

We cannot become better versions of ourselves by waiting for time to pass. Therefore, learning how to manage our time well is essential. Rather, we must use our time wisely and in a way that advances our goals in order to maximise its value. It is clear from research that a person with an uneven time mode is unable to manage learning and development throughout life.

● Insufficient Time for Innovation and Creativity

Innovation and creativity are essential to any business. Most people understand that creative minds need time to unwind, think, envision, and generate ideas. However, ineffective time management typically leaves us with little time for these kinds of pursuits—a busy day leaves little room for imagination and creativity.

● Delaying

The practice of delaying tasks is called procrastination. While there are many possible causes, ineffective time management is one of the key ones. Ineffective time management results in unplanned and unstructured work schedules, which prevent employees from devoting as much time to their essential tasks.

● A lack of self-control

Time management and self-discipline go hand in hand. One of the most common reasons people make up justifications is bad time management. For instance, if they get home exhausted from a hard day at work and don't feel like cooking dinner, they will simply order takeaway. Another instance would be if they were to complain that it was already too late since they didn't have enough time to clean the house or go to the gym.

Because it enables us to control our behaviour and ourselves, self-discipline is an essential part of our lives. However, people who have poor time management are less likely to become disciplined since they are often pressed for time.

Constantly Being Busy

I have witnessed a lot of people who were constantly overworked and kept occupied. I advise you to avoid being one of them. Everyone requires downtime to refuel. Your muscles and brain are similar. Your strength won't increase significantly if you overtrain and continue lifting weights every day because you prevent your muscles from healing and becoming stronger. Your brain is the same. If you don't give it time to heal, it won't perform to its best ability. You might be able to accomplish a few more tasks if you worked seven days a week without breaks or days off, from early in the morning until late at night. However, at some point during the day or week, your level of concentration and the quality of your job will both significantly decline. Pushing yourself won't accomplish anything truly worthwhile; all it will do is make you more stressed out.

I don't intend to imply that you should spend the entire day here. Not at all. I'm trying to convey that, even when you're doing something you enjoy, feeling overworked and overwhelmed can result from not providing your body, mind, and brain adequate time to relax and recuperate.

Recognise that if you don't take any pauses, you will run out of fuel. We will go into more detail about this later, but your brain is not made to be continuously driven without any downtime. All through the book.

Every hour or two, take a rest. Keep yourself apart from your workstation or computer. Step outside and start moving. Take fifteen to thirty minutes to do something unrelated to technology. After an hour or two, return to work, take another break, and resume the process. Additionally, give yourself at least one day off to unwind. For individuals who struggle with it, like me, those "ah ha" moments typically occur when you let your brain heal.

Therefore, even though you may believe that taking breaks isn't particularly productive, in reality, they're You're Only, giving you more chances to record those "Aha" moments. In addition, recovery time allows you to practise new abilities and, of course, refuel your willpower. Even while I know that taking one day off will make me much more productive in the days that follow, I still find it difficult to do so.

Time Theft: The Effects Of Postponement

Let procrastination be your time thief. Even though you know what needs to be done, you simply can't bring yourself to do it. If you put off starting, it will be more difficult to restart later. However, procrastination isn't always a bad thing—there are instances when it might benefit us. For instance, we may put off tasks to rest or concentrate on other things first when we're exhausted or overly busy. But procrastination can become a problem if it keeps us from finishing vital chores and living life to the fullest! We'll examine the causes of procrastination in this chapter, as well as strategies for overcoming it, such as setting daily goals and sprints and avoiding environmental distractions like cell phones.

Procrastination: A self-control issue

Self-control is required to overcome procrastination. Put differently, people who procrastinate are not lazy; rather, they are just unable to control their actions.

Being able to manage your urges and complete things that need to be done is known as self-regulation. This involves putting off tasks until later (procrastination) and using impulse control to avoid temptations that can prevent you from achieving your objectives.

You may master the skill of self-regulation at any age! You may do more with less effort by learning how to better manage your time and energy with practice.

The "why" behind putting things off

You and everyone else who procrastinates do it for the same reason. You believe that things will get better and the task won't be as difficult if you wait.

There are indeed moments when having a different attitude or having less on our minds makes things simpler. It is also true, though, that if we put off doing something, it will take longer later—and even longer if we keep putting it off until a later date. We can finish a task faster if we get started on it early enough. This frees up time for other projects and reduces the chance of distraction.

There is no excuse for procrastinating other than laziness or lack of drive due to the law of diminishing returns, which states that delaying an action causes its effect to weaken with time. "I can't get started because I feel overwhelmed" or "I'm not motivated enough" are some of the things you can tell yourself. However, thinking in this way simply makes things worse because it only gives us an excuse not to start and makes us feel horrible about ourselves when things don't go as planned!

Perfectionism and procrastination

Perfectionism is a form of cognitive distortion characterised by an excessively high standard of self-improvement. "If I can do everything perfectly and make no mistakes, then I'll be worthy of love and respect" is the mentality that underlies perfectionism. However, that isn't how it operates!

Meeting those expectations may cause you to put off tasks because you believe you need more time or assistance than is now available. Or perhaps you just give up on trying because it seems too difficult and frightening. In either case, tension, worry, sadness, and even eating disorders can result from this pattern (particularly when the task at hand involves food).

Because we are always comparing ourselves to those, who seem to be better than us at everything—even though they might not actually be—perfectionism can also lead to low self-esteem because nothing we achieve is ever truly great enough in our view.

You, the workplace, and procrastination

At work, procrastination is an issue. In addition to stress, anxiety, and sadness, it can result in reduced performance and low productivity. Additionally, procrastination might result in health issues like heart disease or elevated blood pressure. Procrastination has far-reaching consequences on your physical health in addition to how you feel about yourself and how other people see you. These repercussions go far beyond your personal life.

Not only do people who procrastinate work that must be done, but they also put their health at risk by delaying sleep for an additional hour of Netflix viewing or worse at night.

Let procrastination be your time thief. It is a widespread issue that has an impact on individuals from various backgrounds and stages of life. In fact, it occurs so frequently that we have a global term for it: "yuck." This is the same word you'd use to describe something repulsive or unsightly.

The causes of procrastination are as different as the persons who indulge in this behaviour. They consist of:

● Laziness (I don't want to do this, for example).

● Fear—for example, "What if I fail?"

Interruptions (such as reminding oneself to check email!)

There are numerous causes of procrastination.

There are numerous causes of procrastination. These are a few of the most typical ones:

● Absence of drive (and self-control)

● Inadequate time management abilities

- Inattention and disorganisation in planning and preparation
- Insufficient energy, drive, and self-control

Things go wrong when we put things off.

Let procrastination be your time thief. It deprives you of the here and now and prevents you from reaching your full potential. Things go wrong when we put things off. Because we believe we will never catch up, it leads to stress, anxiety, and concern. Furthermore, it can be so stressful to complete a project or assignment that we fail to appreciate our accomplishments or look forward to taking on new tasks as a result.

The greatest strategy to beat procrastination is to work towards your objective little by little each day until it becomes ingrained in your routine.

Ignorance is a weak justification for putting off tasks that need to be completed.

- Putting off tasks is a weak justification for procrastination.

- A time thief is procrastination.

It's time to get things done and quit making excuses!

Anything worthwhile to accomplish is worthwhile to do well.

It won't take long for something to stop being a priority in your life if you don't take the time to do it correctly. Your focus and efforts will shift, leaving behind a disorganised heap of unfinished projects, hesitant endeavours, and guilt trails that follow us everywhere we go—even into our dreams. Learn to identify your priorities and set aside time for them every day—one hour on the weekdays, two hours on the weekends, or whatever works best for you—to escape this fate!

Regain control over your procrastination and complete the tasks at hand.

To take charge of your life, you must first recognise the issue. Are you still holding out for the one item that would solve everything? Are you waiting for instructions from someone else?

How can procrastination be recognised? When someone starts something but doesn't finish it, that person is procrastinating. They lack motivation since they are not really committed, which prevents them from acting.

Since procrastinators frequently experience high levels of stress, they might believe that taking a break would enable them to unwind and reduce their tension. This is actually unproductive, though, as procrastination may turn into an addiction that keeps people from completing tasks that are truly important to them or that they truly want to complete (like finishing their schoolwork). Put another way, when we procrastinate, we remain inside our comfort zones rather than venturing outside, where we can discover exciting surprises!

Setting Smart, Visible Goals

Setting goals at an organisation can be challenging, particularly if many people are working there for whom the goals need to be specified. With the greatest of intentions, these goals are often formulated and articulated, but little happens after the initial thrill. Well-aligned goals can provide direction for both companies and their employees. Establishing objectives helps people and organisations understand their purpose and makes it simpler for them to figure out how to follow suit.

What is goal setting exactly?

Establishing objectives can be done on an individual, team, or corporate basis. Establishing objectives means reaching a goal in any form within a given time frame.

Which four objectives make up the core of goal setting?

Setting goals yields four important outcomes: accountability, motivation, vision, and fulfilment (or achievement). These findings support employees in understanding their place in the larger vision, working towards it, and joining the team in celebration when the goal is accomplished.

principal objectives of goal-setting

1. Increasing drive

Establishing objectives could motivate employees to take on projects that seem outside of their comfort zones. Employee engagement is higher when they have a goal to strive for, and studies show that goal-setting strengthens workers' sense of commitment to their employer. This boosts workplace morale and motivates workers to perform better.

2. Pursuing a shared objective

If very intelligent individuals working on the same project produce radically different results, the problem is a lack of a shared vision. By setting both global and micro goals, managers can determine when it's critical to provide feedback.

3. Taking on more accountability

Setting goals helps keep employees responsible. The next stage after creating goals is to evaluate their progress. This way of thinking also benefits managers in remote work contexts by empowering them to challenge employees directly about meeting goals, performance, or anything else relevant.

4. Reaching predetermined goals

The practice of creating goals is the most straightforward and trustworthy way to assess when a project is finished. Remote workers can concentrate on the objectives that clearly define success since they can concentrate on the output that needs to be provided by the deadline rather than worrying about completing their needed number of hours. Reaching objectives can increase employees' sense of fulfilment in addition to increasing overall job satisfaction and retention. This increased loyalty leads to higher retention rates.

Page Six

The Detox of Technology and Time Management: Disconnect from social media and electronic devices on a regular basis. Establish "digital detox" times to help you focus again and minimise distractions.

Effective Time and Energy Management:

Acknowledge that during the day, your energy levels change.

Match your workload to your level of energy.

For instance, set aside your periods of greatest energy for in-depth work and crucial choices.

Time management and decision trees: Make decision trees outlining several scenarios and possible outcomes for complex decisions. This methodical technique can help you make decisions with less stress and in less time.

The Method of "Getting Things Done" (G.T.D.): The G.T.D. technique, made popular by David Allen, places a strong emphasis on keeping all ideas and activities in an orderly system, reviewing them frequently, and setting priorities according to relevance and context.

Time Management for Remote Work: To improve productivity, set up clear lines of communication, define expectations for availability, and create an organised work environment if you oversee or operate remotely.

Effective Time Management for Sales Personnel: Time blocking is one strategy that salespeople can employ for prospecting, following up, and closing deals. Tasks can be streamlined with CRM and lead management solutions that work well.

Time management and time wasters: Determine typical time-wasters and make efforts to reduce or stop them. Overindulgent socialising at work, needless paperwork, and frequent meetings are a few examples.

Time management with Weekly Themes: Give each day of the week a distinct topic. Planning, for instance, may take up Mondays, meetings, and creative work, Tuesdays, and Fridays.

The Principle of "Eating the Frog" and Time Management: Take up your most difficult or disagreeable task first thing in the morning, as suggested by Mark Twain. The remainder of the day will feel easier after it's finished.

Effective Time Management with S.M.A.R.T. Goals: Maintain concentration and clarity by applying the S.M.A.R.T. criteria (Specific, Measurable, Achievable, Relevant, Time-bound) to your weekly and daily goals.

Travellers can utilise applications and technologies to automate itinerary management, track spending, and expedite trip planning. This guarantees that time is spent effectively, whether travelling for work or play.

Time Management for Carers: People who look after kids, elderly relatives, or other people should set up routines and ask for help when they need it. Make self-care a priority to prevent burnout.

Time Management and Visualisation of Objectives: Make visible reminders of your long-term objectives, such as a vision board.

This can act as a motivating aid to help you stay on course.

Time management and Effective Communication: Work on your communication abilities to avoid misunderstandings and to cut down on the amount of time you spend making adjustments and clarifications.

Time management with the "Warren Buffett 2-List" strategy: List your top 25 professional objectives, then rank them in order of importance. Prioritise your genuine priorities by disregarding the other twenty goals and concentrating on these five.

Time management and the "No Meeting" Day: To enable uninterrupted, concentrated work, set aside one day a week, or a portion of it, as a "no meeting" day.

Time Management for Volunteer Work: If you participate in volunteer work, set aside certain times to fulfil your responsibilities and make sure they fit into your calendar.

Time management and reflective journaling:

Keep a notebook in which you consider your everyday activities.

Note any areas that could be used better.

Make plans to modify your time management techniques.

Time Management and Ongoing Feedback: To learn more about your skills and places for growth in time management, ask mentors, supervisors, or colleagues for their opinions.

The "Flow" State and Time Management: Try to get into a state of "flow," where you're totally focused and extremely productive. Determine the circumstances and assignments that allow you to reach this level.

Managing Time and Developing Personal Core Values: Ensure that your everyday actions reflect your basic beliefs. This might give you drive and a feeling of purpose so you can use your time wisely.

Time management and gratitude: To keep a happy attitude and lower stress levels, develop a gratitude practice. This will help you become more adept at managing your time.

Time management and maintaining a healthy balance in your life: Never forget that efficient time management is a tool, not a goal in itself. Creating a balanced, happy life that is in line with your beliefs and goals is the ultimate goal.

REACTING TO CHANGE

Life's one constant is change. The world is always changing—from cultural changes and human development to technical breakthroughs and variations in the economy. The capacity for adaptation becomes not only a desired quality but also an essential talent for success and general well-being in this dynamic environment. This essay examines the importance of change adaptation, its potential difficulties, and the ways in which people and organisations can develop flexibility in order to prosper in an unpredictable environment.

The Need for Adaptation

Things will change inevitably, and it is usually unpredictable. It might manifest in a variety of ways, such as a change in one's circumstances, a global pandemic, a professional move, or a technical advancement. Our lives may be significantly impacted by how we react to these changes.

Resilience: Adaptation strengthens resilience, enabling people and organisations to overcome hardships and disappointments.

Innovation: By promoting fresh approaches to problem-solving and thinking, adaptation promotes innovation.

Relevance: The capacity to adjust guarantees relevance in a world that is changing quickly, both professionally and commercially.

Learning and Development: Getting used to change frequently entails picking up new abilities and information, which promotes both professional and personal development.

Difficulties in Adjusting to Change

Although adaptation has many advantages, there are drawbacks as well:

Comfort Zones: Since change forces people to leave their comfort zones, people frequently oppose it. Although familiarity restricts growth, it offers a sense of security.

Fear of the Unknown: It might be frightening to face the unknown. Fear of change has the power to immobilise people and organisations, keeping them from taking calculated risks.

Impact on Emotions: Adversity can arouse intense feelings like fear, doubt, or even sadness. Managing these feelings and acknowledging them is necessary for successful adaptation.

Resistance: Both personally and collectively, resistance to change is widespread. It may show up as resistance, doubt, or hesitancy to adopt novel approaches.

Developing Flexibility

It is possible to improve and refine adaptability over time. The following are methods for developing flexibility:

Open-mindedness: Adopt a growth mentality that views change as a chance for development and learning.

Lifelong Learning: Maintain your curiosity and dedication to lifelong learning. Seek fresh information and abilities that are pertinent to evolving situations.

Building Resilience: To increase resilience, work on your emotional intelligence, coping methods, and stress management techniques.

Flexibility: Think and act with adaptability.

Networking: Make connections with people from different backgrounds and viewpoints to extend your horizons and obtain new perspectives.

Being ready is trying to anticipate changes and having backup plans ready to lessen their effects.

Organisational Adaptation

For an organisation to flourish, adaptation is also necessary. The following are some methods for encouraging flexibility in a business setting:

Adaptive Leadership: Foster an environment where leaders promote and exemplify flexibility across the entire organisation.

Clear Communication: Clearly and consistently explain the motivations for change attempts.

Employee Involvement: Ask staff members for their opinions and suggestions and involve them in the transformation process.

Training and Reskilling: To give staff members the abilities required in sectors that are changing, invest in training and reskilling initiatives.

Encourage a culture of experimentation wherein measured risks are made to investigate novel avenues.

Getting Input

Acquiring proficiency in check-ins with direct reports

You must discuss your desired working relationship structure in open and honest dialogues with direct reports. You must approach staff management with a coaching mindset as opposed to a traditional one. This implies that instead of just telling them what to do, you'll need to become inquisitive and pose a lot of open-ended questions. You can learn how to offer tailored help to your direct reports by posing open-ended questions such as "What would better support from me look like?" Some may look to you more for advocacy or problem-solving, while others may seek more mentoring. During check-ins, slow down, mirror what they say to make sure you understand, and refrain from mental jouncing when you solicit feedback or hear ideas. Your people must experience validation, worth, and being heard.

Receiving constructive criticism in a work environment where it is not customary might make it difficult to acquire the input you need to advance as a leader. In these circumstances, it may be beneficial to think about getting input from outside sources. These third parties may consist of outside consultants or staff members from different departments who do not report directly to you.

Bringing in outside consultants with experience in team dynamics and leadership development is one approach. These consultants can collaborate with you to pinpoint areas in need of development and get input from your team. They might be viewed as more neutral and objective because they are not affiliated with the company, which could result in more candid and helpful criticism.

Organising skip-level feedback meetings is an additional choice. During these meetings, a representative from a different division or level of the company asks your team members for input on your behalf. If you're worried that team members might not feel comfortable providing you with direct feedback, this can be especially helpful. After that, the person collecting the feedback can consolidate and summarise it for you, making it possible for you to see themes and patterns that you might not have otherwise noticed.

While getting input from outside sources can be useful in some circumstances, it's crucial to employ these techniques sparingly. It could be an indication that more serious problems within the company need to be addressed if your team members feel they are unable to provide you with direct feedback. Furthermore, depending entirely on input from outside sources can act as a crutch, keeping you from improving your capacity to ask for and accept feedback.

They don't cause problems. They are provocateurs.

Observe the people that stir up trouble on your team. These individuals possess the ability to glimpse the Titanic and predict that we will drown before everyone else. Do not write them off or think they are troublemakers. These are the individuals with the depth of understanding and foresight to guide you through a crisis before it arises. Pay attention to their opinions, assist them, and provide resources. Don't undervalue these folks or their abilities. Their criticism is frequently tempered with caution and bravery.

One important component of receiving criticism that we frequently overlook

You'll need to regularly get input from your manager and peers in addition to your direct reports. What happens if someone you respect or someone in a position of authority gives you feedback that is not in line with your values? It's crucial to remain receptive to the criticism, that is, to avoid being defensive and to be unbiased.

Critically and impartially assess the goals and principles that guide the feedback you're getting. I encounter inexperienced managers far too frequently, who are understandably insecure in their new position and hungry for a promotion. They do not use this filter when they receive input from senior staff members. For instance, you might hear from a boss or senior employee that you should hoard authority in order to advance or that your team should produce enormous amounts of subpar work because the business values output over quality. The following filter questions must be applied to this feedback as well as all other feedback:

What kind of beliefs and associated actions is this feedback based on?

Do I adhere to these principles? If not, what steps do I want to take to ensure that my integrity isn't compromised going forward?

Every day at work shouldn't require you to give in on your moral principles and integrity. NEVER.

establishing deadlines and realistic goals

Setting reasonable objectives and due dates is an essential component of efficient time management. We may experience overwhelming or discouragement when we establish objectives and deadlines that are too ambitious or unreasonable, which might result in procrastination or burnout. Setting objectives and due dates that are too close together or too simple, on the other hand, can cause complacency or a lack of drive.

It's critical to first recognise your strengths and weaknesses before establishing reasonable objectives and timeframes. This entails accounting for your skill level, time, and resources, as well as any outside variables that can affect your capacity to reach your objectives.

Setting difficult yet attainable objectives and deadlines is possible if you have a good knowledge of your strengths and weaknesses. Setting deadlines for each work and breaking down more complex objectives into smaller, more achievable ones might be beneficial. This might assist you in tracking your development over time and in maintaining motivation and focus.

It's crucial to factor in additional time for unforeseen circumstances and potential roadblocks when establishing deadlines. To make sure that everyone is on the same page, it's also critical to communicate your deadlines clearly and understandably to any stakeholders or team members who may be affected.

Lastly, when it comes to deadlines and goals, it's critical to be adaptive and flexible. Should you discover that you are invariably failing to fulfil a specific objective or timeframe, it might be essential to reconsider and modify your strategy.

To sum up, realistic goal-setting and deadline-setting are critical components of efficient time management. Setting attainable goals and maintaining motivation and attention while working towards them is possible if you are aware of your strengths and weaknesses, divide more ambitious objectives into manageable tasks, and provide additional time for unforeseen difficulties.

The Advantages of Time Management Skills

As our previous exercises have shown, we probably have some free time and a skill set that will help us create distinctive organisational habits. It's also very probable that you're eager to get going, and that's fantastic! To slightly sweeten the pot, though, here are a few advantages you will soon experience in your life.

The positive feedback loop between time management pro,ductivity and happiness has already been discussed. However, this is more than that. Misra and McKean's (2000) research indicates that stress can be reduced more successfully by time management than by recreational activities. This is not to say, however, that you shouldn't engage in soothing activities. Their research found that a considerable reduction in stress can be achieved by combining anxiety control, leisure, and excellent time management.

Additionally, it is obviously advantageous to know exactly what has to be done at any given time. As we'll go into more detail in Chapter 2, this will represent your priorities. These can (and ought to) direct our time allocation. Including passion-driven activities in your calendar is usually a smart idea because they help you balance your time between productive and leisurely pursuits.

Furthermore, we create room for the people we care about when we give priority to the things in which we truly believe. When interacting with them socially, we can also use some of our enhanced communication skills. This makes it possible for everyone to have clear expectations. We also have more time for the pastimes we think we're too busy for. There are innumerable anonymous surveys asking people what they would do if they had more time. Those who would finally learn German or spend more time with their kids are two common responses. Some people simply want some alone time, a book, and tea. Someone even promised to install solar panels in his backyard so he could use them for an additional fifteen minutes every day! These hopes, meanwhile, seem unrealistic because time cannot be mass-produced in this way.

However, a lot of these idealists have disregarded effective time management. If these goals are significant enough to each individual, then anybody can achieve them. An amazing capacity to prioritise what is worthwhile and what just doesn't come as a result of this. Time management does, in fact, clear up our calendar. Everybody has encountered some form of the idea that we should only keep possessions that make us happy in order to maintain a neat home. The same concept holds for managing your time well, even though life is typically more complex. Increase the activities that bring you joy. Expand on the things you are talented at. There's never enough time for everything. So why not exert all of our efforts?

We'll work together to expand on your priorities in the upcoming chapter. Having a clear vision of our destination will greatly aid in our journey there. We'll also go over how to apply the SMART methodology for goal-setting and how it directly relates to optimising our time. After classifying our outstanding chores using the Eisenhower Matrix and the Pareto Principle, we'll discuss how to monitor our progress and make necessary adjustments to our goals.

OutsourcingAnd Consolidation

Action plan: Determine which tasks you can assign or outsource to free up time for more important endeavours.

In the fast-paced world of today, time is a precious commodity. Whether you are an individual seeking a better work-life balance or a professional, your secret weapon may be the ability to delegate and outsource. You may reclaim hours from your day by using this action plan to discover tasks that can be assigned or outsourced. After reading this comprehensive guide, you'll have the knowledge and assurance necessary to improve productivity, simplify your processes, and focus on what really matters.

Authority Delegation

Delegation is a strategic technique that helps you be a better leader and decision-maker than just allocating tasks. Learn the art of delegation, from setting clear objectives to choosing the most qualified team members. Learn how delegating can help you be more productive.

Selecting Tasks That Can Be Delegated

Not every task is made equal. Determine which duties can be assigned to others. We'll talk about the prerequisites for delegation, such as tasks that are repetitive, time-consuming, or beyond your area of competence. Look for hidden gems that will allow you to have more time on your hands.

The Advantages of Contracting Out

Outsourcing advances delegation by adding outside knowledge. Discover more about outsourcing, from freelancers to specialised businesses. Understand how outsourcing can provide efficient solutions at a reasonable cost while optimising results.

Creating Your Outsourcing and Delegation Strategy

Make a special action plan that satisfies your goals and the resources at your disposal. To ensure success, we'll go into detail about developing a delegation strategy, selecting an outsourced budget, and determining critical performance indicators.

How to Control the Process of Delegation

It could be challenging to delegate without clear guidance. Discover the logical steps involved in effective delegation, including task selection, communication, progress monitoring, and offering constructive feedback.

The Fundamentals of Contracting

With confidence, start your outsourcing journey. Under the title of Outsourcing Basics, this chapter covers finding trustworthy partners, negotiating contracts, protecting intellectual property, and forming long-term collaborations.

Overcoming Challenges in Delegation

Delegation presents challenges. Learn how to overcome common challenges such as trust issues, a fear of losing control, and communication blunders.

Evaluation of Achievement and Continuous Improvement

Record your attempts at delegating and outsourcing. Acknowledge the use of feedback loops and KPIs in achievement measurement. Learn the concepts of continuous improvement so that you can gradually improve your strategies.

True Case Studies

Find real-world case studies of individuals and businesses that have successfully delegated and outsourced. Find out how these strategies altered their business practices and increased production.

Using Your Plan

Apply the knowledge you have just gained right now. Create a detailed action plan that takes into account your goals, available resources, and challenges. Take the first steps towards living a more productive, balanced life.

Delegation and outsourcing are life skills that can help you redefine your priorities and increase your productivity. Equipped with the information and tools in this book, you can take control of your schedule and do more than you ever thought possible. It's time to assign and outsource in order to maximise your potential.

Handling Too Much Work at Once

Having too many things to do is a regular occurrence in today's fast-paced environment.

The following are some useful tactics to assist you in meeting this challenge:

Delegation: Determine which duties can be assigned to other individuals or resources.

In addition to reducing your workload, delegation enables you to capitalise on the skills and talents of others.

Elimination and Simplification: Consistently assess your activities to identify those that can be streamlined or don't make a substantial contribution to your objectives.

Streamlining intricate activities can conserve both time and energy.

Learning to Say "No": Show the guts to turn down requests and assignments that don't fit into your priorities.

By concentrating on what matters most, you'll be able to concentrate on your most significant objectives.

You'll be taking a significant step towards better time management by coordinating your activities with your top priorities.

We'll look at practical tools and strategic planning strategies in the upcoming chapters to help you translate your objectives into actionable steps.

Prepare yourself to make a successful plan and establish ambitious targets.

Methodical organising

The Value of Organisation

One essential instrument for efficient time management is strategic planning.

It enables you to clearly identify your objectives, create targets, and arrange your work so that your time and resources are used as efficiently as possible.

We'll look at methods and strategies in this chapter to assist you in developing a successful strategic plan.

Setting Strategic Objectives

Establishing specific targets that complement your long-term objectives is the first stage in the strategic planning process.

The following tactics can assist you in establishing strategic goals:

Long-Term Objectives: Determine your desired state of affairs over an extended period, say, three or five years.

Set challenging objectives that will motivate and propel your career and personal development.

Short-Term Objectives: Divide your long-term objectives into more manageable short-term objectives.

These intermediate objectives give a sense of accomplishment and progress by acting as checkpoints along the route.

Metas SMART: Make sure your goals are clear and focused on achieving observable outcomes by using the SMART (specific, measurable, achievable, relevant, time-bound) method.

Making a Successful Timetable

A crucial aspect of time management is making an efficient timetable. It entails determining your priorities, allocating time for critical tasks, and coming up with a time management strategy. The following actions will assist you in making an efficient schedule:

1. Establish your priorities: To begin, decide which of your objectives and tasks are most important. These are the most important tasks that need to be completed first and take up the most time.

2. Calculate the amount of time required: Determine the approximate duration of each task. Estimate each task's completion time realistically and provide additional time for unforeseen issues or delays.

3. Make a schedule for yourself: With a planner or scheduling programme, list the times that you will work on each activity. Schedule relaxation periods and breaks, together with time for significant family and personal activities.

4. Employ time blocking: This strategy involves setting aside specified time slots for particular tasks. By doing this, you can make sure that you have enough time to do each activity and maintain your attention.

5. Be adaptable: Keep in mind that unforeseen events could occur, and it's critical to be adaptable with your timetable. Should the need arise, be ready to modify your schedule, and

don't forget to notify anybody who might be impacted.

6. Review and modify your schedule frequently: Review and modify your schedule frequently, if necessary. This can help you stay on course and ensure that you are using your time wisely. For instance, you might estimate that it will take you ten hours to finish a high-priority assignment like writing a report for work. Next, you can make a timetable that allows a certain time for this activity; for example, you could work on it for two hours every day for five days.

To sum up, efficient scheduling is necessary for efficient time management. You may maximise your time and accomplish your objectives by determining your priorities, projecting the amount of time required, creating a timetable, employing time blocking, being adaptable, and routinely evaluating and modifying your calendar.

Methods for Scheduling Time

A common time management strategy is time blocking, which is setting aside certain time slots for particular tasks. The following are some methods for blocking off time:

1. Pomodoro Technique: This method has you divide your work into 25-minute intervals, or "pomodoros," and take little rests in between. After completing four Pomodoros, you take a longer break. By employing this strategy, you can keep your focus and avoid burnout. For instance, you may arrange to answer emails for four Pomodoros in the morning, followed by a lengthier rest. Then, you may plan four Pomodoros for afternoon project work, with a longer break in between.

2. Time Blocking by Activity Type: This method entails allocating time blocks for each type of activity and combining related tasks into groups. One such approach could be to allocate

a specific time slot for responding to emails, another for making calls, and still another for working on projects. For instance, you may set up 9:00–10:00 am for email checking and replying, 10:00–11:00 am for phone calls, and 11:00–12:00 pm for project work.

3. Priority Time Blocking: This method entails allocating time slots for high-priority work ahead of time and then allocating time slots for lower-priority tasks in between. This might assist you in concentrating on and completing the most crucial activities.

4. Time Blocking by Energy Level: Using this strategy, you may plan high-energy and focused work for when you're most alert and focused throughout the day. Less taxing chores can be planned for times when you're feeling low on energy.

5. Time Blocking by Personal Rhythms: This method entails planning time slots in

accordance with your routines and habits. If you are an early riser, for instance, you should plan to do your most critical work first thing in the morning while you are most focused and awake. For instance, you may plan to work on a project from 8:00 to 10:00 am, then take a break. Next, you may plan to work out or engage in a self-care activity from 10:30 to 11:30 am to help you decompress.

To sum up, time blocking is a flexible approach to time management that you may tailor to your tastes and working style. You may stay focused, be productive, and accomplish your goals by employing strategies like the Pomodoro Technique, time blocking by activity type, priority, energy level, and personal rhythms.

An Electronic Work Area

You need the correct management tools to help you stay on top of your work and make sure you are meeting deadlines, in addition to the necessary physical objects for your home workstation. Thankfully, there are lots of digital tools available to assist you in doing this. It is advisable to decide on the management approach you wish to employ before selecting your digital management tools.

The Comprehensive To-Do List

You are asked to break down each item on your to-do list in this manner. When you are starting a project or working on several projects at once, it comes in quite handy. You would make a list of the projects you are working on and then list the tasks you need to accomplish for each project. Then, going one step further, you would give each task an informational assignment. For instance, you might include a list of the sources or documents you will be using to gather information if one of the project's duties was to create a quarterly report. This way, you'll know exactly what has to be done and how to do it when it comes time to finish the assignment. Although it may seem like there are too many lists, this might be an excellent strategy to employ if you enjoy being methodical and organized with your activities. But you also shouldn't devote more effort to creating lists than to working. It is not intended to be a work-related distraction; the lists are there to assist you.

You may find a lot of apps that are useful for these lists. These are essentially note-taking applications that assist you in creating lists. These apps organize your projects and activities in a way that makes them easier to find and understand, making them more effective than a plain notebook and pen. As a result, you won't need to invest hours looking for the appropriate paper. These applications include Apple Notes, Microsoft OneNote, Evernote, Notion, Google Keep, and Obsidian.

Evernote

One of the most widely used note-taking applications, Evernote works with both iOS and Android smartphones. This is because of its general functionality, accessibility, and ease of use. To mention a few, it lets you store notes, pictures, papers, sketches, and scans. All you need to do is start a fresh note for your project and fill it with whatever you choose. You can then designate tabs for this data. Your material will then be arranged based on these tags, which will function as sub-sections. To view a tag, all you have to do is click on a project and navigate to it.

Evernote's search features are also quite good. It will recognize text if you submit a picture or document that contains text. Thus, it can read the image's text and determine what you're looking for if you search for a certain word related to the image. The app's functionality will change depending on the various membership tiers that are offered.

Thought

Notion is a tool for collecting notes, organizing activities, and keeping track of references. It is not only an excellent management tool, but it may also facilitate teamwork among coworkers. Team members can be given tasks to do, and you can make checklists that can be crossed off as tasks are finished. You may even divide your pages into a workspace that contains the pages you share with others and a private page for your work. As a result, nothing is shared, and your coworkers cannot view your pages.

Google Keep

Google Keep is a great software for your lists and notes if you work a lot on Google Drive and store all of your work there. You can save notes and photos from any Google app you use, and it connects to all of your devices with ease. This can also be done with the help of an accessible

Chrome Extension. For the first 15GB, Google Keep is a free application. Should you go above this, further storage will cost money.

OneNote for Microsoft

Because it's a free app, Microsoft OneNote is a favourite among many employees. You can use it to construct divided digital notebooks into pages. If you have a stylus, you may add options to notes, photographs, and even handwritten notes. It's a straightforward, conventional programme that will assist you in managing your workload.

Obsidian

Most people are not familiar with the note-taking app Obsidian. It does, however, include a lot of tools that can help you stay on top of your job and is really helpful. One of Obsidian's best features is its ability to link notes and pages together. For instance, a report you've already written might be useful in an article you're working on. As a result, you can quickly refer to the report when writing by linking it to your article notes.

Notes on Apple

Those who are familiar with Apple products should use Apple Notes. Although it's a free program, it offers all the essential note-taking features you need to make lists. The ability to share notes with other Apple users and connect this software to Siri is one of its nicest features. Though it doesn't arrange notes like some of the other applications on this list, Apple Notes easily stores notes and lets you search for them.

These are only a few of the several note-taking applications that are available. They can assist you in making well-organized and simple-to-follow advanced to-do lists. They'll rapidly prove to be far superior to a pile of notes piled up on your desk.

Make sure the vegetables are readily available, clearly visible, and ready to be used.

For single mothers who are trying to provide a balanced and healthful meal for their family, it is essential to make sure that veggies are readily available, visible, and ready to use. Meal preparation is heavily influenced by convenience in the busy life of a single mother.

The bother of lengthy meal prep can be eliminated, and single moms can save time by keeping veggies readily available, such as pre-cut and cleaned in the refrigerator.

Equally crucial is visibility; when vegetables are easily visible, they act as a continual reminder and promote healthier eating habits. In addition to encouraging improved nutrition, this accessibility helps establish healthy eating habits in kids at a young age by providing a good example.

It also lessens the temptation to choose processed, less nutrient-dense options when time and energy are at a premium.

Eventually, having easy access to veggies can improve the family's general health and support single mothers in leading more manageable and healthy lives.

Adopt a carefree mindset to make the most of the time you spend with your child.

Do you frequently find yourself in a never-ending race against the clock, making an unwavering effort to live up to everyone's expectations?

A situation that many parents encounter is that their drive to succeed can occasionally verge on self-imposed competition. However, it's important to understand that taking a more laid-back approach can reduce stress and increase the likelihood of having deep conversations with your child.

Mothers frequently feel the pressure of society's standards and compare themselves to other women. However, it's important to recognize that this never-ending trying can be emotionally taxing and counterproductive.

Prioritizing the quality of time you spend with your children is just as important as prioritizing how quickly you finish activities despite the temptation to do so. Daily tasks that are rushed through can take away from the important times.

Comparing oneself to other mothers all the time might cause undue stress and feelings of inadequacy. Each family is different, with its own set of circumstances and difficulties. Accept your uniqueness and concentrate on what's best for you and your kids.

You can never replace the priceless time you spend with your children. Perfectly timed breakfast or the Cheerios scattered over the floor can wait. These are the golden years of your child's development, and they won't last forever. Their emotional connection and general well-being should come first.

Adopting a more relaxed mindset has various benefits for you and your kids, such as:

● Decreased stress: Living at a slower pace lowers stress levels, which enhances general well-being.

Enhanced bonding: When you're not always hurrying, you may spend more quality time with your child. Stronger emotional ties result from this.

Reducing the strain that one places on oneself can lead to an improvement in resilience and mental health.

● More patience: Being carefree encourages patience, which helps you deal with the difficulties of parenthood.

● Savouring the present: You can spend more time with your child and make enduring memories by slowing down.

Parenting can be more gratifying and less stressful if the race against time is abandoned in favour of a more relaxed approach. Making time for your child a priority over the never-ending quest for perfection enables deeper bonds and treasured memories.

It's a method that recognises how fleeting childhood is and how important it is to cherish each moment.

Give your kids age-appropriate tasks to complete.

Giving kids jobs to do can be quite beneficial for single mothers for a number of strong reasons. First of all, it gives kids a sense of freedom and accountability while imparting valuable life lessons that will help them as they mature.

Second, it lessens the burden for single moms, who frequently manage a variety of responsibilities by themselves. Age-appropriate duty delegation allows single mothers to free up time and energy for other important responsibilities, including self-care.

This sense of shared duty and belonging can strengthen the relationship between children and single mothers.

Additionally, chores help kids develop important life skills like time management, organisation, and discipline that will help them in the classroom and the workplace.

Essentially, giving kids duties not only helps single mothers by relieving some of the burden off of them, but it also equips kids with essential life skills, strengthens the bond within the family, and lays the groundwork for becoming responsible, self-sufficient individuals.

Be loving and attentive.

It's critical to realise that research suggests teens from single-parent homes may be more prone to melancholy and low self-esteem. But you can significantly reduce these dangers and support your child's mental health by showing them that you care. To elaborate on the significance of love and care:

● Boosting self-esteem: A positive self-image is created when you consistently compliment your child on their accomplishments and hard work. They gain confidence in their skills and feel appreciated and acknowledged, which might improve their self-image in the long run.

● Developing emotional resistance: Your child might acquire emotional resistance with the emotional support you give them by spending time with them and participating in their interests. They come to know that in trying times, they can rely on you for support and empathy.

● Open communication: Comfortable surroundings are created by spending quality time together and engaging in shared activities. When your child knows they have your whole attention and support, they are more likely to confide in you, discuss their worries, and ask for advice.

● Strengthening relationships: Your child and you develop enduring ties via play, reading, and sincere engagement. These ties provide a source of emotional stability, especially in trying or transitional times.

Benefits to mental health: A parent's love and presence are essential to a child's mental well-being. Your affection and attention serve as shields against sadness and low self-esteem, enabling your child to deal with adolescent obstacles more skillfully.

Effective parenting is spending quality time with your child and showing them your affection both verbally and physically. These activities improve your child's mental health in general, as well as their sense of self-worth and emotional stability.

You can give your child the love and support they require to flourish—even in the face of adversity—by consciously working to deepen your link.

The Eisenhower Matrix: How to Use It

The four quadrants of the Eisenhower matrix assist us in prioritising our work according to their significance and urgency. Consequently, we have:

Quadrant 1: Critical and urgent assignments

Important but non-urgent jobs are in quadrant two.

Quadrant 3: Important but urgent activities

Quadrant 4: Important but not urgent tasks

We will next go into detail on how to use this matrix effectively.

Important and urgent jobs are in Quadrant 1.

These are the things that need to be done right now. There are emergencies, issues that need to be resolved, or impending deadlines. Working on these responsibilities as soon as possible is imperative.

You should make a list of all the things that are both urgent and significant in order to use this quadrant efficiently. To keep these chores from getting worse, try not to neglect them and complete them as quickly as you can. Recall that while these jobs typically demand the greatest amount of time and effort, they also typically make the biggest contributions to our overall objectives.

Important but non-urgent jobs are in quadrant two.

The chores in this quadrant don't require immediate attention, but they do contribute to our long-term aims and objectives. These jobs frequently call for preparation and foresight.

It is best to schedule regular time for these duties in order to utilise this quadrant to its fullest. You might need to set out time in your weekly or daily schedule for this. Despite being the most overlooked, this quadrant holds the secret to long-term success, which is ironic.

Important yet urgent jobs are in quadrant three.

These are things that need to get done right now, but they don't help you reach your long-term objectives. These are frequently duties that come from other people, such as phone calls, emails, or interruptions from coworkers.

Developing techniques to lessen these distractions is helpful in efficiently managing this region. To reduce distractions, this could entail establishing boundaries with coworkers and family, scheduling certain times to take calls, or setting up automated email responses.

Quadrant 4: Non-urgent and non-important tasks.

The tasks in this quadrant do not advance our goals and don't require urgent attention. These could be leisure pursuits that don't provide value or tasks that are distracting.

Minimising these chores is key to making effective utilisation of this quadrant. Considering how enjoyable many of these activities are typically (such as watching TV or perusing social media), this might be challenging. But it's crucial to keep in mind that these chores may take up time that you could use for the assignments in Quadrants 1 and 2.

Listing all of your responsibilities and placing them in the appropriate quadrants is the first step in using the Eisenhower matrix. Next, arrange your time and energy in order of each task's priority and urgency. Recall that although this procedure could appear tiresome initially, it will eventually become instinctive and significantly enhance your time management skills.

Taking Command Of Your Life: Techniques For Achieving Your Objectives.

Taking Charge of Your Life, also known as self-governance or self-discipline, is the practice of regulating one's behaviour and decision-making in order to achieve a desired outcome or goal.

One of the key benefits of self-rule is that it allows individuals to be proactive rather than reactive. When people rely on external factors or other people to govern their actions, they are at the mercy of those factors and people.

Another benefit of self-rule is that it promotes self-awareness and introspection. When people are in control of their behaviour, they are more likely to reflect on their actions and decisions and to consider the impact they have on themselves and others.

Self-rule also fosters greater autonomy and independence, as people are able to rely on themselves rather than others to guide their actions.

It can also be difficult to maintain self-discipline and consistency in one's behaviour, especially in the face of temptations or distractions.

To cultivate self-rule, individuals can practice setting and achieving goals, developing good habits, and building self-awareness and self-knowledge. It's also important to set realistic expectations and to be patient with oneself.

Self-rule can also be enhanced by surrounding oneself with supportive people and environments. This can include seeking out mentorship or guidance from people who have achieved success in areas that one wishes to improve in. It can also include creating a physical environment that is conducive to self-discipline and productivity.

In conclusion, self-rule is an essential aspect of personal development and success. It allows individuals to take control of their lives, make choices that align with their values and aspirations, and create the outcomes they desire. However, it also requires discipline, consistency, and patience. With practice and support, individuals can develop the skills and mindset necessary to govern themselves effectively and achieve their goals.

Ways of achieving goals through self-rule

Setting clear and specific goals: It is important to have a clear understanding of what you want to achieve and to set goals that are specific, measurable, attainable, relevant, and time-bound. This helps to provide direction and focus and to make progress more tangible and achievable.

Setting Specific Goals Strategies

One of the most important aspects of setting clear and specific goals is that they provide a clear direction and purpose.

Another important aspect of setting clear and specific goals is that they can help you measure your progress. When you have a clear goal in mind, you can track your progress and see how far you have come.

To set clear and specific goals, it is important to first identify what you truly want to achieve. This may take some time and reflection, but it is essential for setting goals that are meaningful and truly align with your values and priorities. Once you have identified what you want to achieve, it is important to break it down into smaller, more manageable goals. This will make it easier to track your progress and stay motivated.

One key strategy for achieving your goals is to set a deadline for yourself. It's also important to make sure that your goals are challenging but realistic.

Another important factor when setting goals is to make sure that they are specific. This means that you need to be able to measure your progress and know when you have achieved your goal. Specific goals also make it easier to create a plan of action and stay on track.

I remember the day I realized that my life was going nowhere. I was sitting at my desk at work, staring at the clock, counting down the minutes until I could go home. I felt unfulfilled and uninspired. I knew that I needed to make a change, but I didn't know where to start.

That's when I decided to set specific goals for myself. I knew that setting goals would give me something to work towards and would help me stay focused and motivated.

I started by thinking about what I wanted to achieve in the long term. I knew that I wanted to be financially stable, so I set a goal to increase my income by 20% within the next year. I also wanted to be in better shape, so I set a goal to lose 20 pounds within the next six months.

I then broke these goals down into smaller, more manageable steps. For example, to increase my income, I made a plan to network more, attend industry events, and take on additional responsibilities at work. To lose weight, I made a plan to exercise regularly, eat healthier, and track my progress.

As I began working towards my goals, I found that I had more energy and motivation than ever before. I was excited to wake up each morning and take on the day. I was also proud of myself for making progress and achieving my goals.

I found that it was easy to get discouraged when I didn't see immediate results or when I faced setbacks. But, I reminded myself that progress takes time and that it's important to celebrate small wins along the way.

Another challenge I faced was balancing my goals with other aspects of my life. I realized that it was important to be realistic and flexible and to make sure that my goals didn't take over my life.

Now, a year later, I can confidently say that setting specific goals has changed my life. I have increased my income by 25%, lost 25 pounds, and have a sense of purpose that I never had before. I have also realized that goal setting is a continuous process, and I will continue to set and achieve new goals in the future.

I highly recommend setting specific goals for anyone who feels unfulfilled or uninspired. It may be difficult at first, but the rewards are worth it in the end. Not only will you achieve what you set out to do, but you'll also gain a sense of accomplishment and fulfilment that is truly priceless.

Identifying procrastination patterns

Procrastination often lurks in the shadows, camouflaging itself as rational decision-making or temporary delay. Yet, identifying the patterns it weaves into our daily lives is the key to unravelling its grip and regaining control over our time and aspirations.

Recognizing the Signs

Have you ever found yourself repeatedly postponing a task, even though you know its importance? Or perhaps you've noticed a pattern of beginning projects with enthusiasm only to abandon them midway. These are classic signs of procrastination. By paying attention to these behaviours, we can shed light on our patterns and triggers.

The Perfectionist's Trap

One common procrastination pattern is the quest for perfection. Striving for flawless results can often lead to overthinking and excessive planning, causing us to delay action. Ironically, the fear of not meeting our high standards can immobilize us, preventing us from taking even the first step.

The Urgency Illusion

Another pattern is the tendency to rely on urgency as a motivator. Waiting until the last minute to complete a task may create a rush of adrenaline, but it also fosters stress and hinders the opportunity for thoughtful, thorough work. Recognizing this pattern can help us prioritize tasks more effectively and avoid the cycle of panic and pressure.

The Comfort Zone Conundrum

Staying within our comfort zones is a cosy habit, but it can also fuel procrastination. We often delay tasks that push us beyond our familiar territories, opting for activities that require less effort and risk.

The Digital Distraction Dilemma

In today's digital age, the allure of constant connectivity can divert our attention from important tasks. The pattern of getting lost in social media, emails, and entertainment can lead to substantial time wastage. Recognizing when these distractions creep in is the first step toward curbing their influence and reclaiming your focus.

Exercise: Analyzing Your Patterns

Take a moment to reflect on your recent procrastination episodes. Identify recurring behaviours and situations that trigger your tendency to delay tasks. Jot down instances where the pursuit of perfection, reliance on urgency, staying in your comfort zone, or succumbing to digital distractions have held you back. By recognizing your patterns, you're laying the foundation for overcoming procrastination's hold.

Remember, awareness is the first step toward change, and you're already on the path to conquering procrastination.

1. Break It Down: The Power of Chunking

When facing a daunting project, it's easy to feel overwhelmed and put it off. Instead, divide it into smaller subtasks and create a clear plan of action. Completing these smaller steps not only reduces the sense of being overwhelmed but also provides a sense of accomplishment that fuels motivation.

2. Set Specific Goals and Deadlines

Setting specific, measurable goals and deadlines can work wonders in combating procrastination. Vague goals can make it easier to put off taking action. Instead, define your objectives clearly and attach specific deadlines to them. This adds a sense of urgency and accountability, making it less likely for tasks to linger on your to-do list.

3. Utilize the Two-Minute Rule

This prevents small tasks from piling up and becoming overwhelming. By tackling these quick tasks promptly, you'll experience a sense of accomplishment and create momentum to tackle more substantial tasks.

4. This structured approach prevents burnout and keeps you focused during work intervals. Knowing you have a break coming up can also

make it easier to overcome the urge to procrastinate.

5. Practice Mindfulness and Visualization

Additionally, visualization can be a powerful tool. Imagine the satisfaction and benefits of completing the task, which can help overcome the initial resistance to starting.

6. Eliminate Distractions

Identify and minimize distractions that sabotage your productivity. Create a clutter-free workspace and use digital tools to block websites or apps that divert your attention. By creating an environment conducive to focus, you'll find it easier to stay on track.

www.ingramcontent.com/pod-product-compliance
Lightning Source LLC
Chambersburg PA
CBHW052149110526
44591CB00012B/1911